MW01703204

Keep the memories fresh.

Gerry Schwartz

OUR NATURAL TREASURE:
GENEVIEVE KROSHUS

OUR NATURAL TREASURE: GENEVIEVE KROSHUS

Stories collected by Geraldine Schwarz

Photographs by Nan Schwarz
Book design by Jorunn Musil

South Bear Press 2008

Our Natural Treasure:
Genevieve Kroshus

published by
South Bear Press
2248 South Bear Road
Decorah, Iowa 52101 USA
<www.southbearpress.org>

First Edition
Copyright © by Geraldine Schwarz 2008
All rights reserved
ISBN 978-0-9761381-4-3
Library of Congress Number 2007903764

Book design by Jorunn Musil
Photographs on the following pages are by Nan Schwarz:
6, 11, 12, 21, 26, 30, 32, 33, 34, 46, 48, 51, 60, 69, 75, 77, 78 and 79.

With the exception of brief excerpts for the purpose of reviews, no part of this book may be reproduced in any form or by any means, electronic or mechanical, including photocopying, recording, or by any information storage and retrieval system, without the written permission of the publisher.

Prepared through Four Colour Imports, Louisville KY
Printed in China by Everbest Printing Company

Introduction

Genevieve Anderson Kroshus lived all her life in Winneshiek County in northeast Iowa. She was born on her parents' farm three miles north of Highlandville and went to the Kjome School, a one room school just across the creek from her home.

In a family of four boys and four girls she did "everything that needed doing" around the farm. As the oldest girl, she should have been the one to "stay in the house and help Ma," but she always preferred to be "out to the barn—especially when there were dishes to wash."

When her older brother, Truman, went to the Luther College Academy in Decorah, she and her younger brother, Pierce, went along and attended parochial school in the basement of First Lutheran Church, and all three stayed with their grandparents. Later she went to the Red Wing Academy in Red Wing, Minnesota. Music was her favorite subject there, and she always played the "Decorah March" and the "Oneota Waltz" as long as she had a piano.

On June 6, 1917, Genevieve Anderson married Albert Kroshus in the Big Canoe parsonage. They farmed on several different places in the Highlandville area and reared three sons—Jerome, Clifford, and Forrest—and a daughter, Cecil. In the late Fifties they retired from farming and moved into Highlandville. Genevieve continued to work as hard as she had on the farm—helping neighbors, nursing Albert until his death in 1962, babysitting with great-grandchildren, and keeping the coffee pot on for dozens of family and friends.

Our family became acquainted with Genevieve when my husband Dean created South Bear School and bought the old hospital in the center of Highlandville. Some of the residents rolled their eyes at

■ Her voice, hinting of her Norwegian ancestry and a little scratchy with age, rises clearly from these pages and pictures. "Genevieve has lots of stories. Genevieve can always make us laugh."

the thought of long-haired hippies invading their town. But not Genevieve. She and Ines Shuros came right over with scrub rags and mops—the old place hadn't been lived in for years and they knew it would want cleaning. They were excited to have new folks in town—it would give some life to the place—even if it were only during the summers.

Genevieve turned the attitudes of the other Highlandville residents, showing them how to become friends with the art students and teachers. Soon the town was won...and one. Genny (she always wrote it Gené) and Martina Stoen brought frosted ginger creams and a big enameled pot of coffee for the students' morning break. Picnic tables were set up on the lawn for Fourth of July or Any Occasion community picnics.

Genny's kitchen became a warm, inviting spot for most of the 200 students who attended the school during its six years in Highlandville. Of course she had her favorites.

When the school moved to rural Decorah, she admitted she just went home and bawled. "You put Highlandville on the map, and now you've just ripped it right off again!" she told Dean.

When Genevieve lived in Highlandville and cooked coffee for us during a mid-afternoon visit...and made open-face dried beef sandwiches on hamburger buns, and put a bowl of jello and another of potato salad and a plate of two or three kinds of cookies plus some krumkake from the tin in the cupboard—and then apologized because she didn't have much to set out ("If I'd of known you were going to stop by I'd of had something ready to eat,")...she'd tell about earlier days around Highlandville in a way that carried the listener back half a century or more. Her home in Highlandville, where she lived for about twenty years during the Sixties and Seventies, was a slice of an earlier era. Like the

■ The South Bear Art School came to Highlandville in 1970. On the far left is the kiln building which was constructed the second year. The barn served as the pottery studio, and the former hospital became a painting studio, dormitory, kitchen and dining room.

Genevieve Kroshus

Norske language she spoke (brought over by her immigrant grandparents and barely recognizable to modern Norwegians), her house puzzled city-raised visitors. A pump by the back porch supplied water ("the best tasting water around here"), the bathroom was "out south," heat came from an oil-burning heater in the kitchen-dining room-living room—a many-purpose room that felt like home the minute a newcomer stepped into it.

Summer and winter, Genevieve walked daily the three or four blocks downhill, through back yards and across the footbridge (where she usually paused to talk Norwegian to Harold Olson) to pick up her mail at the Highland General Store and Post Office. Usually Martina Stoen, who lived in the former bank, went along and they stopped for coffee at one house or the other on the way back. In slippery weather Genny used her broom to steady her footsteps coming down the hill from her house and would lean it against Martina's house near the door when she got that far. In a phone call, she would say, "If you're coming out this morning, just check and see if my broom is at Martina's. Then I'm either over getting my mail, or at her house having coffee." Mail arrived at her box from all over the world. Peter Deneen started a tradition by sending her a letter from Panama addressed simply: "Genny, Highlandville, Iowa." Many others followed from Norway, Germany, Israel, Korea, and all over this country. They always found their way to her.

Life in Highlandville was comfortable, contented. And all of the thirty year-round residents kept the town pleasant and interesting.

But a time came when Genevieve's sons worried about her being alone in her house, not having plumbing or an easy path to the store. They urged her to move to Decorah, to an apartment in the Oneota Housing Development for retired people. There she had a bathroom and hot running water in the kitchen sink—but she didn't like to wash dishes any more than she ever had!

Sunday afternoon at the Highland General Store. The post office is closed but the telephone booth is open. Have a seat on a bench in front of the store and tell us the news.

Genevieve Kroshus

■ Today and yesterday…not so far apart. The body of today rides in a wheeled chair. The spirit and memories of yesterday soar sharply against the dullness of today's breakfast menu.

Genevieve Kroshus

For nearly ten years Genny lived in her Decorah apartment with her collection of horses—pictures, calendars, tapestries, a china closet full of china horses—plants, her TV (for "General Hospital") and record player (for Lawrence Welk and "Somewhere My Love" from Dr. Zhivago*), her much-used and much-loved telephone, and her round table which was always ready to welcome a visitor for coffee. On many days she would set the table and cook coffee three or four times as different ones dropped in. And as she said, she was "on the go a lot." She always went back to church at Big Canoe on Sundays and for "circle," and, of course, for the Strawberry Festival in June.*

But again her children worried. She fell from time to time, broke some ribs, spent a few days in the hospital. So she moved to the Winneshiek County Care Facility where her father had been superintendent many years before, after they left the farm. Most of the stories which follow came from our visits in her room at County Care.

—Geraldine Schwarz

THAT'S THE BEST nurse here. And she's so strong! She's a farm girl so she knows how to work—and she can lift anything. Working on the farm—that makes a person strong.

I suppose the hardest job I had was pitching hay. Because you had to pull it out from the stack, you know, and pitch it to the cows. And putting the hay up—that was hard, too. They used a hay fork that they'd stick into the load to lift it with a pulley through the big door, and then it would go on a track into the barn. My job was to drive the horses to pull it in, and oh that whiffletree was so heavy. So finally my dad fixed a kind of cart for it, and that made it easier. When that fork of hay was in, then they'd holler, and I'd turn the horses around and go back to pull up the next one.

Sometimes I'd help at the neighbors—not for haymaking or threshing, but milking and chores sometimes. I remember when I was at Gulrud's and the Mr. came home tight. And she said, "You get out there and milk those cows." So she got him kind of headed for the barn, and we went back to the house. After a while she said, "We better go down and see how he's coming." So we went down and there he was, laying in the feedway—sleeping—snoring away. Well the cows were bawling to be milked so I said, "We'll have to milk them."

But she said, "There's one that kicks."

"That's okay," I said, "I can fix her." So we got a rope and I tied it around her in front of her udder and then we tied it around her hind legs and to the barn door. We laughed so to see the way we tied her up. But she never kicked.

I remember one time when Jerome was farming and he was threshing at the neighbors and I was over there helping Kathryn with the chores and so forth because Wanda was taking care of a baby. And I'd said I'd milk the cows, because you know when they were threshing they wouldn't get home until late—sometimes after dark. So Jerome said just to leave that one cow out in the pen, not to put her in the barn because she was a kicker, and he'd milk her himself when he got home. One of the fellows that was threshing with him had to go right past Jerome's on his way home to do his own chores so he stopped in and helped me get the cows in the barn and we left the one out like Jerome said. So then I milked them all and when Jerome got home he said, "What's that cow doing out in the lot?"

And I said, "You said to leave her out because she kicks."

"Well you left out the wrong cow."

Genevieve Kroshus

We always had a dog, of course. You had to have a dog if you were going to farm, because he could save you so many steps. There was one, he was a shepherd, and his name was Shep, too. He lived to be fifteen years old. And oh, he was so smart. He'd go out to the pasture and sort out the milk cows from the rest and just bring the milk cows in. And the kids could do anything and he'd never snap at them or anything. He was really a good dog.

Then when Albert and I were farming, we got a dog from Old Dr. Inman, here in Decorah. It was a grey dog, maybe not just a farm dog but more like a watch dog—a German Shepherd. And he wouldn't let anybody on the place that wasn't supposed to be there. But of course, that wasn't always so good either because sometimes he didn't know who was supposed to be there. Like our neighbor Iver Lundering. He came over every week to play cards, and then we got the dog and he couldn't come on the place until we got a hold of that dog. He didn't think that was so funny. And the dog would go get the cows, but sometimes he did too good a job—put them right through the fence.

I had to laugh at Emma Sollien one time when I was over there and I was talking to her about her dog. "Yes," she said, "he'll go get the cows any time of the day that we want him to. Do you want to see?" Why no, there wasn't any sense to that, bringing the cows up in the middle of the afternoon. But that dog of hers heard her talking and it got right up and went out and fetched the cows.

WHEN MY DAD'S dad came to this part of the country, he hired out—he worked for his cousin that was a Kjome. And so he was called Thurston Kjome. That was the way they did it then—you had to take the name where you were working. And so everybody knew him by that.

(left) The family of Gilbert and Karen Anderson in 1916 shortly before Truman joined the army. Left front are Marie, Trudy, Karen, Gilbert, Kathleen and Genevieve. Behind them are Pierce, Truman and Myron. Collection of Karen Maria Nott.

(below left) Four generations: Gilbert Anderson, grandfather; Genevieve Anderson Kroshus, mother, holding son Jerome Lyle Kroshus; Maria Bakke Nelson Anderson, great-grandmother, in 1919.

(below) Karen Maria Wermager Anderson (1874-1962) and Gilbert Anderson (1867-1958), Genevieve's parents. Married in 1893, they raised eight children: Truman, George, Genevieve, Pierce, Myron, Gertrude, Marie and Kathleen. Long days and hard work have not dimmed the sparkle of Norwegian humor in their eyes.

And then when he married my grandmother, then he had to go back to his real name. And one lady from Spring Grove, she said to my grandmother, "I suppose Anderson is so much swell-er a name than Kjome."

"No," my grandmother said, "it's not that. It's that we have to go by the right name, the one that's supposed to be."

But I guess the woman thought we'd gotten too good for Kjome or something.

AH, ROMMEGROT. We always made that up on the farm with our own milk. We'd run it through the separator so the cream went in the cream can and the skim milk went in the milk can. And then for rommegrot we'd mix it half and half—we made our own half-and-half. And then when you'd cook that and stir it, it would get so nice and thick and that butter would come up on the top all melted. We used to eat cream and bread for supper, just that good thick cream on the homemade bread and Ma's good homemade dried beef. That was a good supper. I get so hungry for that.

Stir the cup of flour into the melted butter to make a thickening. Pour the hot milk into the thickening and stir real fast and real hard until it thickens. If it's too thick, stir in a little half-and-half. Add a little salt to suit your taste. Put a little butter on top to melt. Sprinkle sugar and a little cinnamon on top (not too much). Don't stir the cinnamon in because that spoils it. And you should eat it while it's warm and the butter is nice and melted.

I like sweet soup, too. And of course they could make that here, but I like it the way I make it, and then to eat it when it's warm. That's when it's good. That sweet soup they serve at Nordic Fest, it's always cold, and that's not the way to serve sweet soup.

Rommegrot (Rømmegrøt)

½ cup butter, melted
1 cup flour
1 quart hot milk
sugar
cinnamon

Cook that until it gets kind of thick. I liked it warm—I didn't like it cold, I didn't.

They make that cooked cereal here and it's cold by the time I get it and then they pour that cold blue milk on it. I said to the girl, "I don't like that blue milk—I like cream."

She said, "What's blue milk?"

I said, "You didn't grow up on a farm, did you." No, she said she didn't. I said, "Well, that's why you don't know what blue milk is."

When we milked and separated then we always fed that blue milk, that separated milk, to the calves and the pigs—they did good on that—or we poured it in the barrel with the ground feed and that was swill. I remember one time Mr. Hexom was going away for a couple days and he asked me to milk for him—he had five cows. So I came down to milk and Mrs. Hexom came out. "I can feed the pigs," she said, "I can do that much." So she went to swill the pigs, and she just had a quart container and dipped some out with that and then she said, "Come on and eat!

Sweet Soup (Søtsuppe)

1 cup or whatever comes in a box of that big tapioca—pearl tapioca. Soak that and then cook it until it's shiny
1 cup raisins, cooked with the tapioca
prunes—some like prunes, I'm not so crazy about them myself
peaches—some people use peaches
a little vinegar to give it a good taste
a little salt—not so much you can taste it
sugar

■ Highlandville, Iowa, on a clear summer day in 1904. From left: the Akre house (under construction), home of Sylvia, Norman and their children Joyce and Robert, later Earl Akre and his family, later still Earl and his brother Lloyd Akre. Below the Akre house is the creamery. To the right is Genevieve's home. Below that, obscured by trees is Olaf Mestad's Garage. The mechanic on duty could fix Model Ts and saxophones. Above and to the right are the barn and house of Strinmoens, later Art and Ines Shuros, and later yet Jason Rima and his family and his rabbits. Below Rimas' is Peter Bidne's home, later the home of Henry and Irene Bentley. Joseph Bjerke lived in the little house to the right of Bentley's. Behind the windmill is the house Genevieve and Albert Kroshus moved out of by wheelbarrow. Below the windmill is the Highlandville Hospital, later South Bear School. Below that, the Highlandville bank would be built in 1910, and later it became Martina Stoen's home. To the right of the hospital is the Peterson store. Proprietors Myron and Esther Peterson lived over the store. Below that and to the right, a barn, and below that and to the right, the Olson house—home of Clara Olson and son Harold. Right of that is the Highland General Store and Post Office. Above and to the right of the store is the home of the store owner, originally Charlie Amundson, later Benny Gulbro.

Come on and eat!" And they didn't come—just one pig was there to eat and she was feeding just that one pig. You can't feed just one pig. And she said, "Why don't they come?"

"Oh," I said, "You have to talk Norwegian to them." So I called them—"Poooooie, Poooooie!" and they came right away. She never learned how to do much chores. He was always so good to her. He took care of my cow, too. He said he would keep it there with his cows and feed it and milk it and give me the milk and cream I needed, so that was pretty good. He was always good to me.

ONE TIME WE had a hired man—Clarence Mestad—and he was so mean to my brother Pierce and me. When we'd be out in the barn doing chores and he'd be milking, he'd squirt us with milk. He was so mean. And then one time he was just bent down getting ready to milk and the cow took a leak all over him. And boy, my brother and I laughed—that paid him back for squirting milk on us. And he never brought any extra set of clothes because he stayed at home and walked back and forth. So he had to walk home then and change because he couldn't work like that the rest of the day. But it served him right.

■ Hands that milked and chored and bridled horses…

My hands still fiddle with those bridles still,
the steel bits sliding over the white shining teeth,
past the dark elastic lips and pink tongues
swallowing into their soft throats.

—Joseph Langland
from "A Dream of Love"
(reprinted by permission of the poet)

One cow I had was such a pet. It was a calf that my folks' cow had when they worked here at the County Home, and my dad was so mad because it wasn't Brown Swiss—the cow had gotten away and gotten over the fence—so I got that calf and the kids made such a pet out of it. They led it around and played with it. And then when it was time to start milking her,

Genevieve Kroshus

she was the worst cow to milk. She would kick and kick. One time she knocked me right in the gutter. I was so mad that I got up and hit her with the milk stool and broke it. But I didn't care then, I was so mad. It was a milk stool that Jerome had made in school, too. But I kind of broke her of kicking. So then I got a switch and put it right there beside me when I was milking, and every time she would lift up that foot I'd pick up the switch, and pretty soon she learned. She'd start to bring that hind leg up and I'd tell her, "You put that foot down." So then she'd put it down again.

She was always one to get out of the pen, too, and one time she found a way out of the gate and had just started down the lane, and I hollered at her, "Rosie"—her name was Rosie—"Rosie, you come right back here!" And she turned around and came back into the pen. She was smart.

When we sold her, Albert told the kids she was crying for them. Oh, then they felt so bad, they cried.

MILDRED WAS HERE last Thursday, I think it was. I called her up and said if she wanted to read that letter, I'd found it again. And she'd better come before I lost it again. I lose so many things! It was a letter that her father, Ole Ness, wrote to my father on his fiftieth. It must have been that my dad had said something once about never making any money, and so Ole wrote, "Dear Gilbert, You say you never made any money, but don't you know, you made so many friends. I've made some money, but I haven't done so well in the other department." And you know it was so kind of cute the way he wrote it.

And so Mildred was here to read the letter and she said, "Can I have it? Because that was my dad."

And I said, "Yes, but that was my uncle and my auntie." They gave me that locket you see there in my confirmation picture. So I asked her to make a copy for me, because I want to have that. It's so kind of cute the way he wrote it.

And it was true, too, because he was married twice and that didn't work out just the best. His first wife died in childbirth—they had five girls and then a little boy that only lived a few months, and she died having another boy.

■ Genevieve's confirmation picture, age fifteen. The 16 x 20 inch portrait in an ornate wooden frame hung in all of Genevieve's homes. In her room at County Care it showed the visitors this lovely young woman, another aspect of the one who sat before them talking.

So he said the girls were with him and the boys were with their Ma. But he didn't treat her just right either. She always had to work so hard, and the day before she died, he had her out putting the logs on the saw buck, and then of course the baby was born too soon and….

He took it real hard, you know. They had to dig her up so he could see her again—opened the grave up and opened the casket and I don't know, I guess that satisfied him. And then after his first wife died, he married an old maid—and I think she was always an old maid, I do.

His oldest girl was Melvina and she used to come up and stay with us, but she was scared of everything. She was scared of the calves—when I went out to feed them, they got close to her and she ran for the house—I think anybody who's scared of little barn calves….So then I fed them by myself.

And he had the store out at Canoe, so on Sundays he hauled the groceries out there and he asked me to go along and help. I said, "I can drive, you know."

And he said, "I know that, that's why I asked you to come along." And then I found out why he asked me…because he got drunk in the back room with the fellow that owned the store building and I had to drive home.

And Melvina was so scared I would go in the ditch. "No," I said, "I won't go in the ditch as long as I can see where I'm going. I know how to keep a car in the road." But she was always so scared of everything.

Genevieve Kroshus

OH SURE, NOW that spring's here, the skunks are coming out. I never got squirted with one myself, but one time when we were driving to Spring Grove, one got us. Because a skunk gets on the road and sees the car lights and it'll follow the light. It doesn't have sense enough to get off the road. And you know when the smell gets on the car and the tires and every thing, you just can't get that smell off. It was awful going in that car for a while.

I remember one time the neighbor boy had been over to the neighbors on the other side of us, and he was walking home in the evening with his lantern—kerosene lantern, you know. And there was a skunk following along behind him. And when he turned around and saw that skunk, he commenced to go faster. And, of course, the skunk went faster, too. We were watching him, and it was so blamed funny to see him trying to get away from that skunk. I guess he got home okay, though, because I never heard of him getting squirted.

One time when the boys were trapping, a skunk got caught in the trap—by one leg, you know. And there was no way the boys could get it out without getting hit. But I guess they held out their hat or something and it squirted right into the cap. And I said, "Well, it hit the right place anyway."

HANS JARLAND LIVED there kind of on that corner across and down from the church—back in a ways. We lived just up the road in the place in front of the church, and Hans would come up and ask if there was anything he could do for us—anything we wanted done.

One time he came up and said those other guys were down at his house drinking and tearing up the place and he couldn't get them to leave. Jerome had just come home from Luther League, and he said he'd go and get them out. So he went down there and told them the sheriff was on his way. And oh, how they ran—one went this way and one went that. Casper

■ Just down the hill and across the creek—a peaceful path in the spring sunshine. But at night, with a lantern in your hand and a skunk on your heels…uff da!

Finholt was an old fellow then, but he ran just as fast as the rest. They used to like to go to Hans's to drink because he was a bachelor and he didn't have a wife to make them go home. And sometimes they got kind of rough.

Well, his relatives were talking about how they were going to put him in a rest home—they wanted to get him out of there and then they could sell his place. And he couldn't stand that. I said, "Why should he have to go to a rest home? He's got his own place and he takes care of himself." But they wanted to have that and get the money.

He took his life, you know. And when they asked Mrs. Hexom if they were going to take the casket into the church, she said, "Yes, you bet they are." But then when they buried him, they buried him outside the cemetery fence. That was Reverend Sius that made them do that.

SACRIFICE OF UNCLE HANS

He kept the fires and dusted the sacristy
And rang the countryside to worship Sundays.
He watered graves and even dusted tombstones.
I don't know what-in-the-world he did on Mondays.
(People generally laughed when
they mentioned Uncle Hans.)

He lounged outside the men's room Sunday evenings,
Social with punks who wanted to be social
And still not too religious. He bowed goodnight
To the last host, and part of the week, he rested.
(How much of the week, I wondered,
when I thought of Uncle Hans.)

He never married, but he kept one cow,
A couple of goats, litter of pigs, some trapgear,
Some whiskey for when the church got cold and lonely,
And a spry brace of horses he drove everywhere.
(My, what a time we planned,
waiting for Uncle Hans.)

He came to clear the downlogs from our timber
One winter in his sleigh; he looked so rosy
My brother said he must have nipped his whiskey
And swallowed half the bottle when he broke her.
(Even those who disapproved
allowed that to Uncle Hans.)

He came with sleighbells ringing in the roadways
And went with laughter bouncing in us children,
Until my father cut the rope that bore him
Off to the graveyard he had kept so tidy.
(No use in laughing, then,
when they mentioned Uncle Hans.)

When the bells rang, Old Hans was in the tower,
And all the ladies' socials on the lawns
Were placed there by his hands. My, off he went,
And no one put a stone where he had gone.
(Most of the stones I knew
were set by Uncle Hans.)

Our weekly confidence held no account
With such extravagance of early rest;
So the local mortuary took his litter
Of pigs, goats, and cow, and did their best.
(No one ever seemed to do
as well as Uncle Hans.)

But I saw Old Hans hanging from his shed beams,
Dangling beyond the lantern light that found him,
And lying beyond the scripture that we read him.
Some think it isn't so, but he sleeps soundly.
(St. Paul and the others tried,
but they didn't know Uncle Hans.)

He had a heart, well, more than he could afford.
If many things he did didn't seem quite right,
You knew he was always giving, if you kept any score.
And Lord, how jolly! Well, let him sleep for a while.
(I'll not say any more, now;
you see, I loved Uncle Hans.

Except that I've got to add that when he was hanging,
Purpled and swollen with scorn, nothing we knew
From prophets to Plato to psalms and Luther and back
Seemed of much use. But I won't let memory go.
(It's the best good thing we have.
I remember my Uncle Hans.)

—Joseph Langland
from *The Sacrifice Poems*
(reprinted with permission of the poet)

■ Joseph Langland is reading his poetry to the students of South Bear School and to some of the community members in the summer of 1975 with the cattle listening only a few feet away.

■ The Kjome School, a stone's throw from the Anderson farm. But reverence for history prevents these stones from being thrown. During its more than seventy years of education, hundreds of neighborhood children ran their hands over these stones, peered from these windows, played Run-Sheep-Run in this school yard.

MRS. CASTERTON—when we were girls—she was my seatmate in Norwegian School. We had Norwegian School, parochial school, for six weeks in the summer at the Kjome school. So we were trying to think of something to do and we decided to wash our desks. But how would we carry the water? So we thought we'd go out to the pump and get our mouths full of water and we'd have our rags all ready when we came back in. Well, I went out first and everything went okay, and then she went out. I turned around to look at her when she got about halfway back to her seat and she burst out laughing and the water went all over the floor. Of course, she could laugh at anything.

Esther Troendle, I remember, was one teacher we had. She walked to school and it was quite a ways for her. That one winter, I know, we had so much snow and she walked ON TOP of the snow banks. And after she got there, then it was to build the fire. But finally she got a neighbor boy to build the fire for her because it got to be a little bit too much for her.

And there was one boy, I don't just remember his name, but he was awful bad. She took her pointer to him—finally broke it on him! And it was a real nice pointer, too. All carved wood.

Emmett Volding and Carl Sella sat behind me, and they were so mean! I wore my hair in braids down the back, and they would reach under the desk and pull my hair. That Carl was so mean! But he was kind of babyish, too. When he was a great big fellow, he would sit in his father's lap—he looked so kind of foolish.

I was homesick so much when I went to school in Decorah, too. We had parochial and English together there—in the church basement, you know. And we'd go home weekends.

But sometimes my dad couldn't come and get us and so it would be awhile before we'd get home. I remember one year we couldn't even get home for Christmas. And OH I was so homesick. But Dad had so many chores to do, and you know it would take a long time to bring the team clear to Decorah, and I suppose the roads weren't the best either. So we had to stay. It was my older brother Truman—he was going to Luther—and me and Pierce—we were going to the parochial school. We boarded with our grandparents, but you know sometimes when you live with your own folks like that, it's harder.

The poor old fellow who taught Norwegian School (like Bible School now, you know)—he taught six weeks here at the Kjome school, and then he went on and taught six weeks at

■ The Anderson farm home, birthplace of Genevieve in 1895 and her father in 1867. When this photo was taken in 1990, her cousin Milford Solem and wife Gertrude were farming the land, keeping the paint shiny white and the plastic butterfly well fed.

another school and then on to another school, all summer. And I always felt sorry for him because he didn't have much. So when we went to church on Sunday, I'd say, "Pa, can we give a little extra so Josendahl can have some?" When you gave the offering at Highland Church, everybody walked up front and put their offering on the communion rail. And then there was a little table off to the side where you could give some to the teacher, and that was the only way he was paid, you see.

He lived there in that house behind Big Canoe church and he walked to whatever school he taught in. He had three daughters and they were musical. One was an organist. Of course, he played, too. And one day he was helping me with something I was singing—accompanying me—there at the church, and his daughter came in and said, "You get out of here now!" Like that. To her own father! Oh, I felt so sorry for him.

■ Highland Lutheran Church, a little north of the Kjome School. Genevieve was one of the first babies baptized here. Through the window, one can see a little table spread with coins for Josendahl.

■ Eighty-four years of glasses—the first year trying to lose them, the rest trying to find them. They helped the eyes see right through a situation and focus on the humor.

Genevieve Kroshus

I WORE GLASSES since I was ten years old. I think it was to Spring Grove we went to get them, I believe it was, and I had to have them put in old frames. Not old frames exactly, but they'd belonged to someone else, somebody in the family. Oh, I hated that because they were these old silver frames and they weren't just so stylish, you know. But that's what we had to do to make it not so expensive.

And uff! I hated those glasses in those frames, so I left them in the barn, I did—upstairs in the barn. And then my mother said, "Where are your glasses?"

"I don't know where I left them." But she kept after me until finally I had to come out with it and go and get them. I wanted the glasses that didn't have any frame, I did. That was the newest kind then. But the folks said no, that wouldn't do for a kid because that kind would break too easy. And I guess probably they were right because I wasn't just too awful careful.

DAD ALWAYS LET us take the horses anytime we wanted to go anyplace—we could always take any of the horses. We could hitch them up to the buggy—we had a buggy—or we could ride—I always liked to ride, I did, because you could go there faster, you know. But my favorite horse, it was the one I rode all over...well, the hired man rode it over to help the neighbors, and the road had frozen into ruts. And don't you know the horse fell and broke its leg. And so there was nothing to do but shoot it. Well, my dad couldn't do it and the hired man couldn't do it, so they got the vet to do it, but I think he almost couldn't do it either. It was such a good horse.

And we had a "spait," but she didn't have a white face. But she fell and broke her leg and we had to kill her, too.

We had one horse that was a Morgan—Morg, we called him. And when I was riding him, I'd say, "Git there!" and he got there, too, you bet.

Mrs. Takle, the dressmaker, was out and she had to get back to town so she was going to take the team, but I said, "You'll have to watch out because one of those horses is balky." "Nay, then what shall I do?" "Why, you can do the same thing I do," I says. "You just wait for him to start up again."

One time Margaret and I were up to Solem's playing cards. And I don't know, maybe it got kind of late, so we drove the team home and put them in the barn. And the next morning when my dad went to the barn, one of them was dead. He said, "What did you do? Drive that horse to death?" But they were both okay when we put them away.

Another time one of the horses stepped on a nail. It was limping around and the kids didn't know what was the matter with it, so I said to bring it up to the house and I'd have a look at it. And as quick as I picked up its leg and looked at its hoof, I could see the head of the nail right there. So I got the pliers and pulled it out and then I put some liniment down that hole and I got a pail of warm water and put some vinegar in it, because they said that would be good for it. And pretty soon that horse was walking around as good as ever.

I did fix a broken leg once though. It was when one of the kid's lambs, oh, I don't know what happened, but it broke one of its front legs. And the kids felt so bad, and I said to bring it in the house. So I took a shingle and broke it in slats and made a splint-like out of it and held it on—wrapped it around and around the leg with pieces of an old sheet. And don't you know it wasn't very long before it was getting around okay. Because it was young, you know.

■ Genevieve made this portrait of her horse, Toby, for a school project when she was about sixteen. She painted on silver-colored foil, probably using the tempera paint available in schools in the early 1900s. Collection of Karen Maria Nott.

G.A. ANDERSON.
1908

Genevieve Kroshus

YES, I DROVE. I drove Model T's, I did. My dad used to sell them and so he'd take me along to drive the new cars up to the farm. And then they'd come there to pick them up—those that had bought them from him. He took me because I had learned to drive before the boys did.

The first car he got, he got as trade for a team of sorrels. We had 22 horses at one time. He always raised five or six colts every spring and then it was to break them and match them up in teams and then sell them. And that's how we got our first car. And I remember we were driving to Spring Grove and I said, "Let me drive."

And Dad said, "Wait until I learn how first."

I knew how to handle a gun before I was 14. The first time I shot a rifle, my auntie showed me how. She was proving up a claim in North Dakota—Williston—and she always had a gun with her. She said she'd teach me how to shoot, so we went down to the creek bottom and I shot. I hit a cow right in her hoof. I guess it didn't hurt her—she just shook her foot a little and went on.

■ How many horses does it take to work a 1908 farm? Ten. Two to pull the manure spreader and eight more to fill it up. Genevieve counts the horses held by Truman, Myron and Pierce as their father, hands on hips, stands proudly before his new barn. All the horses had names, of course, as did Shep, the dog.

By 1923, when this photo was taken of Big Canoe Church, everyone seemed to be driving a car. But in 1910 when Genevieve was learning to drive, necks at the church must have craned when she motored up.

TODAY IS Kathleen's 50th wedding anniversary down in Charles City and I wish I could go, because you see I was 19 when she was born so I kind of helped raise those younger ones.

It'll be this afternoon at the church and her, we say "adopted daughter" is putting it on. See that's Cecil's oldest. We call her Dutchy. Her real name is Karen Maria. Real Norwegian. When she went to school, the teacher called her Karen.

"No that's not my name," she said. "My name is KAARen MARia." She was just a little bit of a thing. But then they got to calling her Dutchy, I can't just remember why. Cecil was married twice, and so the younger kids have the second dad. And Dutchy was quite a bit older, so sometimes she'd go to stay with my sister Kathleen, because Kathleen didn't have any kids. So then she got to be kind of like Kathleen's daughter.

A handsome couple. Albert Kroshus married Genevieve Anderson in June, 1917 in the Big Canoe parsonage. They reached their forty-fifth anniversary before Albert passed away in 1962. Celebrating a fiftieth was a goal not many couples lived to reach.

FORREST HAD A turkey once that he got when he was working on the road. One place had a lot of turkeys and they said this one was going to die because the other turkeys were pecking at it, so somebody should take it.

So Forrest said, yes, he could take it. And he brought it home and tied it up to the tree. And pretty soon the kids were out there playing with it and making a pet out of it. I said, "I'll butcher that turkey for you."

"Oh, no! You can't butcher our turkey," the kids said. But I told them that was no way to do—they couldn't have a turkey tied up to a tree. So I butchered it for them and I suppose they all ate it. But the time Cecil had the lamb—these people had sheep, it was a brother and sister that lived near us when we lived on the Hanson place—and they gave Cecil this lamb. And of course it was such a pet, but it jumped over everything, jumped over the fences and JUMPED RIGHT INTO MY FLOWERS and ate them! So I said I would butcher it. Oh no, I couldn't butcher it. But you know that was no way to do—you couldn't keep just one lamb around. So I butchered it. And then we were having cold tongue for supper and Cecil wouldn't eat. Wasn't going to eat her lamb's tongue!

ONE NIGHT THE Bidnes brought supper down when Albert was sick—it was the night before he died—and they brought down this nice roast beef dinner. They had bought Bruce's 4-H calf and the meat was so good and so tender. And so we were eating it and Bruce came in, and I said, "Come on and have some of this roast beef, it's from your 4-H calf." And he turned right around and left. They get so attached to those calves, you know.

■ The Kroshus family in June of 1941 as Jerome was about to leave for the service. Clifford, Jerome and Forrest are seated, with Cecil, Albert and Genevieve behind them. "Genevieve didn't brag on her kids, but you knew she was proud of them all the same."

Genevieve Kroshus

AND I MADE lefse, and I made fattigmann. Oh that fattigmann was so good. I get so hungry for things like that, but of course all we have here is macaroni and nooooodles. Uff, I get so sick of that. If they'd let me in the kitchen, I'd make up something, I would.

Lefse

(This is Ida Saquitne's recipe—we used the same one.)
6 cups boiled potatoes, riced and cooled
1 stick butter (I used oleo) melted
2 cups flour
a pinch of salt
powdered sugar

Make it into a ball and then roll it out real thin. Cut it into diamond shapes—make with your knife first one way and then the other to make diamond shapes. Put a little slit in the middle when you put them in the hot fat. They fry up real fast, and then you take them out and put a little powdered sugar on. For Christmas you can sprinkle a little colored sugar on them, too, if you want to.

Take about a third of a cup of dough and roll it out real thin. Put that on the lefse pan—it's got to be nice and hot—and do both sides, and then dust it with a little powdered sugar.

Fattigmann, you know, it's just the egg and the flour and just a little sugar, and then you roll it out about this thin and cut it diamond shaped and fry it in the hot fat, and you put them in about this big and then they spread all out when they're frying. And they're just crisp and good.

Fattigmann

2 eggs beat real good
a little vanilla—it wouldn't be any good without vanilla
flour enough to make a dough so you can roll it out

Lutefisk? Ya, we always had lutefisk for Christmas and all. One time I was invited out to Forrest and Evelyn's, I don't just remember if it was at Christmas—just Sunday dinner, I think it was. And they had lutefisk and potatoes and lots of other things, too.

And Vickie had one of her friends home with her from college, and this girl had never had lutefisk before. So Forrest said, "You can just try it and if you don't like it, that's okay because the cat can have what you don't eat." So the girl, she tried some, put the melted butter over it and fixed it all up and took about one bite. No, she didn't like it. So they put it out for the cat. And don't you know, the cat licked all the butter off and never touched the lutefisk!

I had an awful time learning how to make pie crust. But Ma, she kept right at it until I learned, because you'd have to, you know. I'd try it so many times and I'd almost bawl because I couldn't get it right. But finally I got so I could do it. Oh, I wouldn't say my crusts were ever just so swell, you know, but they seemed to go okay.

You had to take the lard and put the flour in there and then crumble it up with your fingers until it was real fine, and then you kind of make it into a ball and then sprinkle the cold water on it until you'd get it so you could roll it out.

We made all kinds of pies. Apple—we had apple trees and the neighbors had a lot of trees, so we got apples from them. And cherry. The neighbors had cherry trees, or sometimes we'd buy the cherries in town. And lemon—I liked lemon pies. And chocolate. Raisin, too, and banana cream. I can't just say I was ever so crazy about banana—I still don't care much for bananas.

And then in the summertime when we had strawberries, we'd make strawberry pie, too—out of the fresh berries, you know. We made that for the Strawberry Festival at the church in June.

Genevieve Kroshus

I EVEN HAD a trained toad once. And, uff, I felt so bad when she died, I almost cried. Albert was going down in the cellar, and I said, "Watch out for my toad."

"I won't hurt your toad," he said. But when he came up, he let the cellar door down, and just then she jumped up on the door jamb and got smashed. Uff, I felt so bad. Because she was just like a pet, you know.

When I would mow grass, she'd hop along behind me, follow me all around the yard. And you know how steep that yard was, so I'd stop and rest a little, and she'd look up at me and wink. And then she'd say, "Gulup. Gulup." Honestly she was so blamed cute, just like she was talking to me. So I talked back to her.

I'd let her in the summer kitchen—she'd wait at the door and I'd let her in there. I didn't let her in the house, but I could have because she was real clean. She'd want to get in—she'd kind of wait around the door, but I didn't let her in. When I'd go in the house, she'd hop right up on the porch and wait for me to come out again. But she really liked to go down cellar. So I'd open the trap door and she'd hop down each step and wait for me to open the door into the cellar.

And then one night Albert was sitting there in the kitchen and he said he was hungry—he'd like a meat sandwich. "Well," I said, "you'll have to go down cellar to get the meat." Because you see we didn't have any ice box. And I said, "Don't hurt my toad." Then the next morning when I opened the cellar door, there she was, smashed flat. But I never heard of a trained toad before. She was such a pet.

■ What a beautiful sound the words "cellar door" have! What a cool, rich entry they recall. Except for the trained toad.

Genevieve Kroshus

I ALWAYS MADE 75 krumkake at a time and then I put them in boxes and used them for Christmas presents, I did. When I was in the apartment, of course, I made them on the gas stove there. And out in Highlandville after we got the gas stove, that's what I used.

But of course the best ones were the ones I made on the old cookstove, because you could get that just right with a few sticks of wood and then they always turned out so crisp and nice. But it got to be too much for me to chop the wood, so then we changed to the oil burner and the gas stove. But me, I always liked the cookstove best.

When we were up on the farm, I believe that was when we lived by the church, and we always got our own wood from our place—down timber and like that. And Ted Gjere came to saw—he had a sawing rig with that round blade—and Clara Mestad and I, we were the only ones there to hold the wood, so we were the wood cutters that day. And you know that was quite a thing to do because you had to hold up those logs, one on one end and one on the other, and put them through the blade. The old fellow that was living there, he came out and said he could help. "No, you can't. You go right back in the house. You'll get into the blade and then we'll have an awful mess." Because you know he was so wobbly and fumbly. And then another time I was the only one there to help and Ted Gjere and I, we sawed the wood, just the two of us. And after that he always called me his wood cutter, and whenever he'd see me, he'd say, "When are you coming to help me cut wood again?"

And then of course after it was sawed, it was to split it, and uff that was a hard job. I remember Jerome would split all the wood for the whole winter. He'd come home from college on weekends all fall and split the wood for us. He'd put up enough for all winter.

■ A bundle of slab wood waits above Genevieve's house for her sharp ax and a trip to her cookstove. Soon the smells of woodfire and fresh krumkake will fill the air.

■ Genevieve sits at the round, solid table in her kitchen—cookstove ready for baking, oil stove ready for warmth, smiles ready for everyone. Photo by Steve Buck. Vase by Tommy Sandoe.

Then after we moved into Highlandville, we of course didn't have any timber, so I bought a load of slab and that was real good firewood. It was only about this thick and it split real easy. So they'd come and drop it off up above the house—they had it on a dump truck-like and they'd just tip it off. And if you could get it split and stacked before it snowed, you'd have some real good firewood. I always made the wood pile up there above the house and I covered it all up except just the little place where I was getting it out to use, so it stayed nice and dry. I carried it down in the wheel barrow, and that was all down hill so it went along pretty good.

The Highlandville home of Genevieve and Albert from the downhill side. Supper was cooked, eaten, and discussed in the room on the left with the double window. The "front room" on the right was for visiting with company, for playing the piano, and for nursing the sick.

I never liked coal. Oh, I'd get a bag every year, so in case you needed a real hot fire, but I didn't like it. Because it was so dirty! Every time you touched it, you'd come up all black and that was such awful stuff to get off, I've never seen anything like it.

I always made krumkake for Maynard Pierce, and he liked the ones that were browner, so when I made it I always got some that were browner—you always do, you know—and those I'd put in the box for Maynard. And for Inga and everybody.

Krumkake

1 egg
¾ cup sugar
1 cup cream
1 ¼ cup flour—supposed to be, but I used less, maybe one cup
½ teaspoon baking powder
a pinch of salt
1 teaspoon vanilla

You have to heat the krumkake iron up and then put about a teaspoon of batter on and bake it first on one side and then turn it over and do the other side. It takes some doing to know just when to turn it over, but after you've done a few, you get so you know. And then you take them off the iron and roll them on the krumkake stick and that makes a nice cone shape. And that one time when George Kjome was having coffee with us, and those girls from Luther College had never had krumkake before and he said, "Look out, girls!" Because you know, if you don't eat them right, they break all over.

WHEN I HAD tonsillitis, my dad had Dr. King come out—he had the hospital there in Highlandville, and people said, "You aren't having Dr. King, are you?" My dad said he sure was. When Myron was sick with typhoid fever, Dad had Dr. King come out and he cured him. But he was a little bit tricky, too. He'd charge mileage, so when he'd come out, he would drive way around, to make it farther.

JEROME AND KATHRYN got Kavin down in Des Moines—that was in February. And as soon as Kathryn saw him, she knew he was the one. He was always such a cute little fellow. I remember when he came out to stay with me and he said, "Grandma can I sleep with you?" And I said yes, he could. So he crawled in with me, but I watched his eyes and he didn't go to sleep for the longest time. He was thinking about something.

And then one morning when he got up, he had wet the bed. And so he got the scissors and cut that part of the blanket out. Jerome and Kathryn laughed so about that. Because it was pretty smart of him to cut that out so we wouldn't see it.

And then when he got in school, he got so he didn't seem happy. He didn't want to play ball or be in the band, and so Kathryn sat him down and talked to him about why he didn't want to be in those things. And he said, "It's because I'm adopted," and he didn't think he was wanted.

"Oh, but don't you know I wanted you SO much and I waited SO long, and as soon as I saw you, I wanted to take you home SO much," Kathryn told him. And then he brightened right up and he was a different boy.

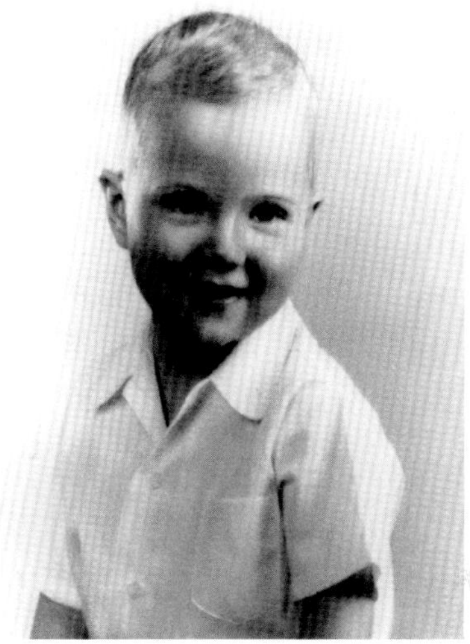

■ Kavin Kroshus at age two, a lively lad for Jerome and Kathryn and a favorite of his grandmother. "I guess they were all my favorites, really."

■ Joyce Akre just back from a successful fishing expedition with Abba. Clara's cats are probably lurking behind the shed.

WHEN JOYCE, Sylvia's daughter, was a little girl—she wasn't in school yet—and I said to her, "Now if you get lonesome up there or they aren't good to you, you can come down here. So one day here she came, and she had her suitcase. And I said, "What happened?"

And she said, "They scolded me." In her suitcase she had two night dresses for herself, and her doll and her doll's clothes.

And another time she had to stay with us because someone was sick, and so we turned the cane couch around toward the wall so she wouldn't fall out. She said, "But I have to get up in case 'Abba' (that was what she called Albert) needs a drink of water." And every time he woke up, she got up and gave him a drink of water.

Then in the morning she was getting ready to go home and Albert said, "Now my night nurse is going on day duty." So then she went home and took care of her father.

She loved to take care of Abba. One time she was up on a chair and I asked her what she

After a hard morning of fishing, a person needs a little time out. Abba and Joyce take a watermelon break.

was doing. She said she was cooking wieners for Abba. And I said, "Aren't you afraid you'll get burned?" No, she wasn't afraid. When I'd wash clothes and fold them, she'd stand right beside me and fold all his things, and she knew right where they went in the drawers upstairs.

He gave her an overall for her birthday. She had wanted one because that's what he always wore. And she got lots of nice things for her birthday—a nice slip and a dress. But she just put them in the corner, and the only thing she wanted to wear was that overall. And she wanted a snuff box to put in the pocket because Albert always had a snuff box, a snoose box we called it. So he cleaned out an old one and gave that to her, and she went around in her overall with the snuff box in her pocket. Oh, she was such a cute little thing.

And then one time when she was visiting me, it was time she should take a nap, so I said, "Should we take a little snooze?" And she ran to get her snoose box! Now wouldn't that have been something?!

Robert and his sister Joyce—they were just like my kids, because when they lived up there behind us, our kids were all grown and so we needed some little kids around. Joyce, she was so cute, and she liked to come visit. She'd leave their house and they'd say, "Where are you going?"

"Going to visit Abba," she'd say. And she liked to go fishing with Albert, down to the creek. I gave her my big straw hat to wear to keep the sun off, and there they'd go, down to the creek to fish. I called them Mutt and Jeff because he was so tall and she was so little. So when they came back I asked her if they got any fish. Yes, they got some catfish.

■ Not to be outdone, Robert Akre has pulled in a pair of trout from North Bear Creek. The Old Rubberneck would really stretch to get a look at these beauties.

Well, I knew there weren't any catfish in that creek—they were just suckers. And Albert knew all the kinds of fish, so where'd she get the idea that they caught catfish? I said, "Are you sure they were catfish?"

"Yes," she said, "We fed them to Clara's cats." And those cats got so they'd watch, and when those two went fishing they'd wait for them to bring back some fish—some of those cat fish.

Once when Robert Akre was little, I was going over to the store and I asked him if he wanted to go along. Yes, he wanted to go. So we walked over, and on the way back we walked past Louis Grindeland's—he lived there in the bank—and he was such a nosey one. He was always one to sit there in front of his big window, and whenever anyone went past, he got up and s-t-r-e-t-c-h-e-d to look. So he did that when we walked past and I said to Robert, "Did you see that old rubberneck?" Yes, he said he saw it.

When he got home he went running to his dad and said, "Do you know what we saw down by Louis Grindeland's?" No, his dad didn't know. "We saw an old rubberneck." Then his dad laughed! Because he knew exactly what we saw.

THAT'S JASON RIMA. I call him my black-eyed beauty. He has such black eyes and real light hair. They lived there in Art Shuros's house and he used to come over to visit me, and he was so cute.

Once he brought over this pail, and he had brought a little rabbit to show me—they raised rabbits in cages, those real nice ones. And he put the pail on the table. So I said, "You better not put it on the table because he might fall off."

“Oh, no, he won’t fall off.” But he moved the pail down to the floor. And then pretty soon he said, “Well, I better take him home now because I think he wants to see his daddy.”

■ “My black-eyed beauty,” young Jason Rima. An expert on rabbits and on entertaining his neighbor.

And I said, “Does he have a daddy?”

And he said, “Don’t you know that?”

“No, I don’t know anything about rabbits.”

“Well, of course he has a daddy, else how would there be little rabbits?”

One time when Forrest was working on the road, they were grubbing out trees and they came up with a baby raccoon. So Forrest brought it home in his lunch pail and gave it to Bruce. And that little thing was so blamed cute. And smart. It followed Bruce around just like a dog or a cat.

But then of course it got big and it should go back to the woods. So Evelyn took Bruce and the raccoon out, way out, in the car. And they were gone quite a while and they all three came back. They just didn’t have the heart to leave it out there.

So it stayed around a while longer, and then it kind of went out in the trees there, and every once in a while they’d see it or hear it there in the woods. Forrest was afraid it would come back and get the chickens, he was. But I guess it never did.

THAT NURSE, she likes to learn to talk Norwegian. So one time she asked me how you say "hind end" in Norwegian. And I told her "bakende." So she was in here and bumped into something and said it was her "big bakende," and then she saw that Jerome was sitting here—she hadn't noticed him before—and she was so kind of embarrassed.

But I said, "Don't mind about that because he has one too. And he knows how to say it in Norwegian, too," I said. That's all the kids talked at home. They learned English when they went to school, same as I did when I went, and same as my folks did, too.

■ Douglas Peterson and Michael Snitker were daily visitors at the art school. They were put to use as errand runners, snack fetchers, and postal delivery men.

No, you weren't supposed to dance and you weren't supposed to play cards either. But we did. We played Flinch. One time we were at Martina's and we wanted to play Flinch, but we needed somebody else to play, so I said we should ask Harold Olson to play. "Oh, do you suppose that would be okay?" Martina said. Why sure it would be okay. So we asked him. Well, he didn't think he knew how to play cards. "Why sure you know how, because your mother always played Flinch."

So he came over to Martina's and we were playing and he was sitting so he could look into her bedroom, and he said, "Martina, that bed looks like it would be big enough for both of us." And then he laughed! And Martina, she was so embarrassed.

We use to play Flinch with Clara Olson, Harold's mother. One time I remember we played until four in the morning. It was Clara and Nora Thoen and Sylvia Akre and me. And then we had to walk home after that. So Sylvia and I walked Nora home—she lived over the other side of the creek, and then we walked ourselves home.

Sometimes Dorothy would play, but we didn't like to play with her so well because she cheated. She'd finish and say she was all out of cards—that's how you win, you know, when you play your last card—and then we'd look and she'd have a whole lapful of cards. We'd say it in Norwegian, "Ah, Dorothy, you've got them all in your lap!"

We were over to her house playing and her neighbor stopped in and he said, "Oh, are you having a card party?"

■ It is always useful to know more than one language. Some things are just funnier in Norwegian.

And the mister said, "No they're having a fart party!" Because she was always such a one to do that, too.

We were up at Spring Grove for the Syttende Mai, and Dorothy let one out, and Mrs. Strinmoen said, "Dorothy!" and Dorothy said, "Oh what's the difference!"

And she was so tight! She would never give a person anything. She asked me to come over and wash her ceiling. I think it was in her parlor and her dining room, it was a big ceiling. And when I got through, do you know what she gave me for pay? A roll of toilet paper! She said, "This is all I can give you until my ship comes in." But her ship never came in!

When we moved from the place up by the store down to the place we bought, I moved everything in the wheelbarrow. And that was not easy because that road wasn't good. It wasn't used much and it was awful rough, and of course it was up to the house and then down again. But I moved everything on the wheelbarrow except the stove. I even moved the china closet. And so when Dorothy wanted to move, she asked me if I would do it. And I said I didn't think I could because she had that ditch there in front of her house. "Oh, sure, you can do that," she said.

So we loaded the wheelbarrow, and you know it tipped over with the table on it, because it wasn't balanced right. We came around the corner of the house and down it went. So then we had to put the table back in and pack a lot of stuff on top of it. And when I got all through moving her, she said, "Well, I'll give you something when my ship comes in."

■ Norwegian Bridge—the best way to get from Genny's house to the post office because Harold Olson would call out, in Norwegian, from his porch, and a few jokes and laughs (in Norwegian) would be exchanged. Oh, you didn't HAVE to speak Norwegian when you were on that bridge, but you just sort of did. Drawing by Larry Welo, reprinted with the artist's permission.

But I guess her ship never came in, because I never got anything. By heck, I thought that was kinda tough. But then one time she asked Irene Bentley to hem up her dress, and she wrote out a check for five dollars for that. Of course Irene wouldn't work without pay. But five dollars just to hem a dress!

THEY STARTED those dances there at the schoolhouse—that was that Torres that started those. He played the accordion—"squeeze box" we called it. Martina and I walked over the first few times. One time, you know, Dean asked me to dance, so we waltzed around a little. And the next day Irene said, "I heard you were dancing." She said so kind of sour, "How's the dancer?"

I said, "He's all right, I guess." I wasn't going to let her get the best of that one.

Earl and Lloyd ALWAYS went to the dances. One of them would bring a box of cornmeal and right in the middle of the dance, he'd spread it all over the floor—so people could slide easier, he said. Mostly just made a mess. Lloyd said he only danced with college girls. "How do you know they're college girls?"

"Oh, I ask them."

"Yes, but don't you know they probably tell you they're college girls just so's they can dance with you." He didn't know what to think about that.

But you had to feel so kind of sorry for them. They'd come down for coffee just about every day, and one day I was just about out. "I guess I'm just about out of coffee. I have to BUY that,

■ The Highlandville Dance–a thirty-year, once a month tradition...and continuing...as long as the fiddlers play, the floorboards hold, and the plaster stays on the walls. "The Dance," a print by Carl Homstad, reprinted with the artist's permission.

you know." So the next day here came Lloyd with a pound of coffee. And I don't know how long he thought that would last because I don't remember that he ever brought another one. And I'd always give them something to go with it, because they didn't have much, you know.

So one day I'd made doughnuts, and I put a plate of those on the table. Lloyd, he took a couple bites and got a funny look on his face. "What'd you fry these in?"

"Lard. I always fry doughnuts in lard."

"They taste like the animal."

"Well, don't eat them then."

Sometimes he'd bring a loaf of white bread down and then I should make a sandwich for him. "Well, yes, but something has to go IN that, you know. You can't just make a sandwich with bread." But I felt so sorry for them because they didn't know how to fix for themselves very well.

One time Earl said that Dean had stolen his family Bible. "Stolen the Bible!" I said. "He never did such a thing." Well, Earl said he knew it was gone because he could see by the dust on the table that it had been there, and now it wasn't!

And when Kim from Korea was living out there, he went up and helped them clean. Well, he was the only one that was cleaning, you can bet. So he carried out everything and scrubbed the floors. And then they carried it all back in—garbage and everything. Made Kim so mad!

You know one time I asked Lloyd what day his birthday was. And he said, "Well, I'm not real sure. If there's thirty days in August, then it's the thirtieth. But if there's thirty one days, then it's the thirty-first." At least he knew it was the last day!

And then one time there was a doings of some kind down at the school—picnic or something, I suppose—and Lloyd had his camera and was taking pictures of everybody. And somebody said, "Say Lloyd, when you get those pictures finished, I'd like to have a copy of that one."

"Don't have no film."

Earl worked at that chicken place in town, and he'd bring home chicken and cook it. And one time he got sweet on a girl at one of the dances, and he told her he'd bring chicken over and cook it for all of them—she lived with those people out at Springwater. Told her what day and everything, I guess.

So he didn't just get the chicken, he went and bought a grill and the charcoal and everything. And so then he got there and got it all ready and they never came home—they were all gone to town. And he came back here and was telling me all about it. "And she was such a nice girl and I think she really liked me."

"Oh, you just forget about those girls," I said. "You've got no business with them anyway." Because you know his wife was out to the County Home.

"But I'd just like to have somebody to hold."

"Well, you just pick up that cat of yours and hold it. You won't get in trouble that way."

Lloyd had a job in town too, one time—at that lawn mower place. But then he came down to my place crying. "What happened?" I said.

"They fired me." They said he wasn't quick enough, and I can believe that, all right.

And, of course, they didn't EVER clean. Sylvia would come out and look at that place—it had been so nice when she lived there—and it just made her sick. We went there one time, that was maybe right after they took Earl's wife to the Home—she got real bad—and we were cleaning up and washing the windows. And Earl, he didn't know why it was so bright in there. "Well, you have to wash the windows, you know. That's the only way you can see out of them."

And then one day Lloyd was down for coffee, "We moved upstairs."

"Oh?" I said, "Why did you do that?"

"Got too dirty downstairs."

"Yes, but what will you do when the upstairs gets too dirty?"

"I s'pose we'll have to clean."

THEY WERE REAL busy up at Peterson's store and they had to go to a funeral, so they asked if I could help out. So I did everything just like they did. But then a fellow from over by Quandahl came in with eggs and he wanted gas. But the electricity was off, so I couldn't pump any gas for him, and he needed gas to get to town, so I gave him the money for his eggs and then he could get the gas someplace else.

So when Myron came back, I told him what I had done, and he said, "What are you doing? Trying to run my business for me?"

And I said, "No, I'm not trying to run your business, but the electricity was off so he couldn't take out his egg money in gas."

A quiet day at the Peterson store in 1990. But the store is open, the lights are on, and Esther will sell you a bottle of Spring Grove pop, some onion-and-sour-cream potato chips–and some trout spinners, if you like.

A lively day at the Peterson store as seen by painter Paul R. Smith while he was artist in residence at South Bear School in 1974. The store is humming and Myron is inside ringing up the sales. Reprinted with the artist's permission.

And so he started to get real mad, and then his wife came in, Esther, and she said, "What's going on here?"

And I said, "He's accusing me of a lot of things."

And she said, "Myron." And he went right out of there.

I never was afraid to talk back to Myron Peterson! One day I was talking to Tinka Selness—she was sitting in the car waiting for her husband to go into the store. She said, "If they sold beer between here and Quandahl, I suppose he would have to stop there, too!"

And Myron walked past us and he said, "You big shit!"

And I said, "Well, you're the biggest shit that ever walked in Highlandville!" And he walked right up into the store. He never said another word. I think maybe he liked it.

Mrs. Brady lived in the big house and she was such a nice clean person. And she came over one time and wanted to pick berries for me. She went way up here and picked berries and way over there, and she went to Borghild Rauk's and picked goose berries for her. And then she was down in the yard washing onions, and Myron came past and he started to get smart with her because he thought she was trying to get sweet with his father. And she took that pan of onions and water and threw it right in his face. I thought that that was the best! Of course, she had to pick the onions up later...but that really shut him up.

And then one time Borghild and I were picking chickens. We were out in her yard and we had overalls on because we had to be catching the chickens and everything. And Myron went past and he said, "You big a-double-s!" Just like that. And I said, "You big belly." Because you know he had that great big belly. And he didn't say anything back. If he had, I would have had plenty more to say to him. I was never scared to talk back to Myron Peterson!

I LIKED TO make those frosted ginger creams—they were good for a crowd. I remember when the school was going on in Highlandville and the students would have some time in the morning kind of like recess, I suppose. So I made the ginger creams and Martina had the big coffee pot, so she cooked the coffee, and the students they really liked that—ate all the crumbs and everything.

You mix the sugar and shortening first and then add the eggs and beat that good. Then you sift the flour and soda and salt—I guess you could put the ginger and cinnamon in the sifter, too—and then add a little of that and a little of the coffee and molasses mixed together, back and forth like that. And then the vanilla. And then you bake them in a jelly roll pan at 350 degrees; you just have to kind of watch them until they're done, it doesn't take too long. When they cool, then you can spread a little frosting on them and cut them in squares. It's just a powdered sugar and water frosting, kind of thin.

Frosted Ginger Creams

1 cup sugar
1 cup shortening (half butter and half oleo)
2 eggs
2 ½ cups flour
1 teaspoon soda (sometimes if the soda is a little old, I put in more)
salt
1 cup of hot coffee
½ cup molasses
1 teaspoon each of ginger, cinnamon, vanilla

■ Painters, potters and poets savor ginger creams from Genevieve and coffee from Martina, whose home in the bank building is in the background of the lower right photo.

THIS LIFE! I'll tell you, you can just have it! I sure never thought I'd wind up in a place like this! People hollering all the time and coming in my room. That's the worst. They come in here all the time and if I'm not here they go through my stuff. That one over there, she's the worst. She came in here and took my cookies and ate them. And she's not supposed to have them because she has diabetes, you know. Yes, she took the cookies. They were these wafers—I'd asked Evelyn to pick up a package for me, and I put them here in this cabinet, and when I went to get them, there were only four left!

Well, the nurse had seen her in here, so I asked her, "Did you take my cookies?" No, she didn't take any cookies. "Well, I know you did, because they saw you."

So then after a while she confessed that she had eaten them. "But I'll pay you for them."

"Well, then go and get your money right now before you forget," I told her. Maybe if she pays for them she won't be stealing again. That's what I hate worse than anything, that stealing. And lying. And she's supposed to be such a good Catholic, too.

After the first time she stole my cookies, well, I was going through her room to get to the bathroom, and she said, "That's my bathroom, you're not supposed to use that."

And I said, "Well, I guess I am because I always have used this one."

So when I came out, she said it again, "That's my bathroom."

"Well," I said, "those are my cookies. And I KNOW you're not supposed to be into them." So that shut her up. But then she said she was sorry she'd taken my cookies and she'd pay for them. No, I said, they'd been paid for once and that was enough. But she should not get into

things that didn't belong to her. No, she wouldn't, she said. But then she went and got into them again, so then I said she should pay. I don't know, maybe she'll learn to keep her hands off other people's stuff.

If I could just lock my room when I go down to the dining room or to the bathroom! But no, they say they can't have locks on the doors, and I don't understand that. I don't know what I did to end up in a place like this. I must have been awful bad to be sent here. Because it is, you know, it's just like a prison! You can't have your own stuff around you. Everybody has to have the same bedspread and blankets and pillow. I said, "I can't sleep on that old stuffed pillow, I want one of my feather pillows." But they said they didn't know what happened to them. That's the trouble, you know, all the things I'd saved, all gone, and I don't even know where.

When they told me I was going to have to stay here, I said, "Well, I'm going to have my chair and I'm going to have my TV." But when the woman comes in to clean, she snorts around about all the furniture in here and having to move it all. "Well, that's what you do," I told her, "because that's what I always did when I mopped. I always moved it around to clean under it, and I don't know why it should be any different here."

■ Genevieve's father's sturdy barn with double rock walled foundation and thick vertical wooden siding stood fast for at least eighty years. But on the day of her funeral, a violent north wind loosened and scattered the foundation stones. Like them, our memories, stories, laughter and tears lay tumbled at our feet. The making of this book helps us to right them.

Genevieve Kroshus

Genevieve Krochus died on March 12, 1990, at the age of 94. The Iowa March winds blew so hard on that day that they caused the rock work on the barn her father built to loosen and fall, scattering on the ground below.

At the funeral in Big Canoe Lutheran Church, Mavis Arneson sang "Den Store Hvide Flok," *the Norwegian hymn sung traditionally at funerals.*

And the wind whipped the group of mourners who went from the funeral at Big Canoe Church to the cemetery across the road. "Nature's pruning shears" broke dry branches from the trees near the graves and sent them tumbling past the headstones as we lay to rest our beloved natural treasure.

■ This tintype of Gilbert Anderson, Genevieve's father, was made in the Dakotas in the 1880s—when buffalo coats and Stetson hats were "all the go." Collection of Karen Maria Nott.

Afterword

Like thousands of Norwegian descendents who grew up in the New World, Genevieve was pleased to find the treasures that her relatives had brought from the Old World had been carefully preserved and displayed at the Vesterheim Norwegian-American Museum (just 14 miles from her home) in Decorah, Iowa. There Gené (as she spelled it) could see models of the sailing ships similar to the ones her father and grandparents had crossed the Atlantic aboard, handcrafted tools and utensils, and exquisite decorative patterns on clothing, containers and cookie presses.

■ Shown here are various historical artifacts from the Vesterheim Norwegian-American Museum. Folkedahl Ale Bowl donated by John Haltmeyer as a memorial to Adaline.

There Genevieve could also show her grandchildren the "rosemaler trunks" (as Joe Langland liked to call them) that those immigrants had packed with clothes, utensils and memories made in Norway. Even though she never saw the land of her father's birth, she could envision his young life there by entering the exhibits of homes, crafts, and daily life in the nineteenth century. And she could revisit scenes from her own youth in the schoolhouse, the church, and other immigrant structures.

■ Below is a typical Norwegian immigrant's trunk, effusively handpainted with decorative floral designs called "rosemaling." Appropriately, when Jorunn Musil designed the dust jacket of this book (left), she chose to use patterns derived from rosemaling.

■ Unless otherwise noted, all photos on pages 80-87 were provided by the Vesterheim Norwegian-American Museum and are used with its permission. Pictured above, it is the oldest, most comprehensive museum in the US dedicated to a single immigrant group. Founded in 1877, it now occupies 16 historic buildings in downtown Decorah, Iowa, and includes more than 24,000 historic artifacts. Vesterheim means "western home." For further information, visit its web site at <http://vesterheim.org>.

THERE ARE few, if any, more vivid accounts of the immigration of Norwegians to the American Midwest than "Norwegian Rivers," a poem by Joseph Langland, who grew up on a farm not far from Highlandville and went on to become Professor of English at the University of Massachusetts. In 1974, when he delivered the Luther College Commencement address and received the Doctor of Humanities *honoris causa*, he recited this unforgettable poem.

Genevieve Kroshus

Norwegian Rivers

Yah, they are so kind of restless,
rushing around hills
and tumbling the polished stones;
they always have somewhere to go.
Even when they pause in precipitous valleys
they climb into deep long cold lakes
and then, again, begin
rapidly falling.

Yah, we have seen them
pouring off mountaintops
like the first dream of a second flood.
Now, one hundred blood-years later
they amaze Norwegian-American travelers,
sailing the bird-like ferries
toward the evergreen towns
or running through summer on the cliff-hung roads,
with the sheer bravado of their origins.

Yah, now shall they see,
the affluent grandchildren,
how strong and supple minds
ran the rebellious rivers into the sea.
And now, yah, shall they hear
the low music of springs
watering the impoverished mountain meadows.
Then let them guess as they can,
yah,
how the terrible excitement of alienation
fell on the manhood of our great-grandfathers
and the playfulness of their children,
and rose in a heartbreaking cry from their limbs
and washed from their empty hands.

Then, yah, it was then,
stout in their sadness,
they stuffed their childhood into rosemaler trunks,
clamped them with iron bands
locked, once and for all, on the eastern hemispheres,
and down the rutted trails and noisy rivers
out through the western fjords,
they rode for half a century over the Atlantic
on one great ascending wave
toward the virgin hills and the wide inland valleys
of Iowa, Minnesota, and Wisconsin.

And now, yah, even now,
grandmothers sitting in their rocking chairs
and watching their children's children
in Bergen and Decorah, Hardanger and St. Paul,
say, half to themselves,
yah, they are so kind of restless,
they always have somewhere to go,
hearing under their vaguely troubled
half-drooping eyelids
the melancholy of hard hills
and old stones
and rivers calling under the walled-up fjords
to the muffled horns of the sea.

—Joseph Langland
(reprinted with permission of the poet)

■ The Schwarz Family in 1972 during Nordic Fest in Decorah, Iowa—Jason (almost 3), Gerry, Sheela (almost 1), Bill (10), Lane (6), Nan (almost 1), Gunnar (8) and Dean Schwarz. Bill began studying pottery in Highlandville in 1974 when he was 12; the others began their study after the school moved to rural Decorah. The whole family often shared picnics and morning breaks with the students and Highlandville community, and Jason headed straight for Genny's or Martina's home. In the scramble of putting kids in cars for the ride to Decorah, he was left more than once and was only discovered missing after the 14 mile trip home. He had begun learning to speak Norwegian and hadn't missed us at all. Photo by Joan Liffring Zug Bourret.

How this book happened—

The beginnings of this book go back to the summer of 1970, when an art school known as South Bear School was started in the small rural community of Highlandville, Iowa (population 30). Among the most interesting residents there was Genevieve Kroshus. A descendant of Norwegian immigrants, Genny welcomed the long-haired newcomers and urged the other residents to become friends with the school's faculty and its students (who numbered 200 in the six years that the school was there). It was during those Highlandville years that writer and literature professor Geraldine Schwarz developed a friendship with Genny, a bond that would continue until Genny passed away at age 94 in 1990. This book's text is based on Gerry's reconstruction of her many conversations with Genny. Nan Schwarz sometimes went along, and photographed Genny as they talked.

In early 2008, having finished the research and writing, Gerry Schwarz approached an old friend, Roy Behrens, for advice on the book's production. Behrens, who teaches graphic design at the University of Northern Iowa, offered to art direct his students in designing the book and preparing it for printing. Each of the twenty-two students in one of his design courses proposed an interior layout and a dust jacket for the book. From those, the work of one was chosen. That student was a talented young undergraduate named Jorunn Musil, and it was she who then took on the task of designing the entire book. Only later did we learn that she too is a decendent of Norwegian immigrants.

Acknowledgements

For their contributions to this book, South Bear Press is grateful to the Vesterheim Norwegian-American Museum in Decorah, Iowa; the late Joseph Langland; photographer Nan Schwarz; book designer Jorunn Musil; and Roy R. Behrens, owner of Bobolink Books, and Professor of Art (graphic design) at the University of Northern Iowa; and the students in a course he taught in the spring semester of 2008.

Among the students in that class were (in alphabetical order) Tiffany Batchelor, Amber Bush, Krista Cary, Tasha Fedler, Shanna Floy, Patrick Fowler, Brennen Gibson, Kayla Grunder, Nathan Hauser, Samantha Hoffman, Laura Huisinga, Alyssa McMahon, Alyssa Mehmert, Katharine Messerli, Jennifer Meyer, Jorunn Musil, Candice Nielsen, Jared Rogers, Mackenzie Schmidt, Rachael Thorne, Beau Van Sickle, and Jodi Williams.

Additional copies of this book can be ordered directly from the publishers at South Bear Press, 2248 South Bear Road, Decorah, Iowa 52101. For further information, visit their web site at <www.southbearpress.org>.

OTHER BOOKS FROM SOUTH BEAR PRESS—

■ *Marguerite Wildenhain and the Bauhaus: An Eyewitness Anthology*. Dean and Geraldine Schwarz, eds. Designed by Roy R. Behrens. 11 x 8.5 ins. 770 pp. 837 illus (402 bxw, 436 color). ISBN 978-0-9761381-2-9. Clothbound, $75 plus shipping.

South Bear Press books can be purchased at Amazon.com (new and used), or go to www.southbearpress.org.

THIS IS A phenomenal archive of the life and work of master potter Marguerite Wildenhain, as well as of the origins of the European concept of *Handwerk*, the role of pottery at the Weimar Bauhaus, and the continuing, prospering legacy of studio pottery in Europe and the U.S. Contains scores of Bauhaus-related images, interwoven with essays, memoirs, diaries, letters, interviews and other candid, written texts, many of which are published here for the first time.

American Craft Magazine
(June-July 2008)—

Those wishing to reconstruct both the European milieu that shaped Wildenhain's work and its fruition on American soil, will find an embarrassment of riches in [Marguerite Wildenhain and the Bauhaus].

Beverly Sanders,
Senior Editor

■ *...that We Look and See: An Admirer Looks at the Indians.* Marguerite Wildenhain. John Nellermoe and Dean Schwarz, eds, with photographs by David Stone. 11 × 8.5 ins. 127 pp. 85 illus (bxw drawings and photos). ISBN 0-89279-025-3. Clothbound, $30 plus shipping.

TO MARGUERITE Wildenhain, drawing was an indispensable resource, for teaching as well as for learning. In the first part of this book, the reader sees the world through the "eye-pencil" of this remarkable artist. Reproduced are figure and landscape drawings that served as inspiration for her own pots. She also helps to understand the importance of drawing to potters and other artists. In the second part, she uses her drawings to share her lifelong discoveries about Native Americans. Her rhythmic observations are those of an admirer who, since childhood, had been driven to know and to understand.

Her [Marguerite Wildenhain's] *presence, her message…are inspiration not only for potters, but for workers in all pursuits. It is rare to have one's life touched by a master.*

Emily Peel

■ *MARGUERITE A Diary to Franz WILDENHAIN.* Letters in the form of a diary, by Marguerite Wildenhain. Dean Schwarz, ed. Designed by Deb Paulson, with photographs by David Cavagnaro and woodblock prints by David Kamm. 11 x 8.5 ins. 125 pp. 70 illus (bxw and color). ISBN 0-9761381-1-5. Paperbound, $40 plus shipping.

IN ADVANCE OF the Nazi invasion of the Netherlands, Bauhaus potter Marguerite Wildenhain (a French citizen, of Jewish ancestry) was separated from her husband and did not know his whereabouts. During part of that time (especially as she traveled slowly across the U.S.), she made drawings and letter-like entries to Franz in a diary of sorts. This is the first publication of those unforgettable pages.

South Bear Press books can be purchased at Amazon.com (new and used), or go to www.southbearpress.org.

RELATED TITLES FROM BOBOLINK BOOKS—

■ *False Colors: Art, Design and Modern Camouflage.* Roy R. Behrens. 9 x 6 ins. 224 pp. Illus (bxw). ISBN 0-97132-440-9. Paperbound.

THIS IS an engaging and often amusing account of the little known use of artists, designers, and architects as army, navy, and civilian camouflage experts (called *camoufleurs*) during World Wars I and II. Described and illustrated are documented attempts—some ingenious, some absurd—at "fooling the eye" by prominent artists from France, England, the U.S., Germany, and other countries.

■ *Cook Book: Gertrude Stein, William Cook, and Le Corbusier.* With visual poems for Gertrude Stein. Roy R. Behrens. 7 x 5 ins. 96 pp. Illus (bxw). ISBN 0-97132-441-7. Paperbound.

THIS IS a biographical sketch of one of Gertrude Stein's closest, most loyal friends, a largely unknown artist named William Edwards Cook (1881-1959). Born in Iowa, he left the U.S. in 1903 and lived overseas for the rest of his life (in France, Italy, USSR and Majorca). It was Cook who taught Stein how to drive, and it was he who also commissioned the then unknown young architect Le Corbusier to design a starkly Modern home (called Villa Cook), the "first truly cubic house," near Paris.

These and other titles from **Bobolink Books** can be purchased at Amazon.com (new and used), or go to www.bobolinkbooks.com.